The Building of Stratford-upon-Avon

First published in the United Kingdom in 1994
Alan Sutton Publishing Limited
Phoenix Mill · Far Thrupp · Stroud · Gloucestershire

First published in the United States of America in 1994
Alan Sutton Publishing Inc. · 83 Washington Street
Dover · NH 03820

British Library Cataloguing in Publication Data

A catalogue record for this book is available from the British
Library.

ISBN 0-7509-0559-X

Library of Congress Cataloging in Publication Data applied for

*Cover illustrations: front: The Almshouses, Church Street;
inset: Shakespeare's Birthplace, Henley Street, rear elevation.
Back: Holy Trinity church from across the Avon.*

Typeset in 11/14 Times.
Typesetting and origination by
Alan Sutton Publishing Limited.
Printed in Great Britain by
Ebenezer Baylis, Worcester.

Contents

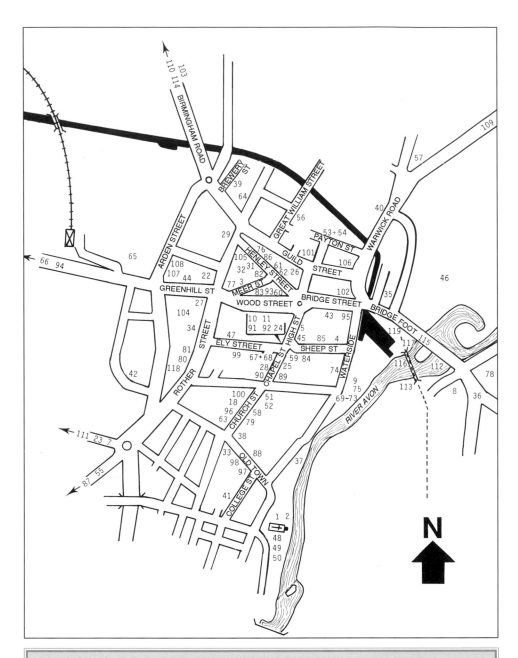

Map of Stratford-upon-Avon. The numbers on the map relate to caption numbers

Introduction

The towne of Stratford stondithe upon a playne ground on the right hand or ripe of Avon, as the water descendeth. It hathe 2 or 3 very lardge stretes, besyde bake lanes. One of the principall stretes ledithe from est to west, another from southe to northe.

John Leland, *c.* 1540

The attractive Warwickshire market town of Stratford-upon-Avon is one of the world's most famous tourist destinations – not because of its own intrinsic merits but because of the enduring fame of its celebrated son, William Shakespeare. To appreciate the architecture of any town it is usually important to try and forget the rich and famous associated with it, but in Stratford the influence of that one man is everywhere. Even 150 years ago it was recognized that 'a great source of the prosperity of the town is the constant influx of visitors to a spot hallowed by so many associations with the name of our great national bard'. Since then the Shakespeare industry has flourished and continued to be an important part of the local economy. Directly and indirectly, it has also affected the way the town looks. Yet take away Shakespeare and Stratford is still an historic town in its own right, with its own character, commerce, and culture – as well as a rich and varied architectural heritage.

By the time Shakespeare was born in Henley Street in 1564, there had been a settlement at Stratford for at least a thousand years. Its Saxon name means the place where a Roman road, or street, crosses the river by a ford – in this case where a minor road linking the Foss Way at Eatington with the Ryknild Street at Alcester crossed the Avon. The position of this ancient ford

1 Shakespeare was buried in the chancel of Holy Trinity, now a place of pilgrimage for lovers of literature the world over. In this early nineteenth- century engraving his wall monument is suitably lit. At this time the church was in very poor condition

2 By the end of the seventh century there was a Saxon monastery at Stratford, probably on the site of the present parish church of Holy Trinity, seen here in an early nineteenth-century engraving. In the foreground is the lock on the then still-navigable Avon

is thought to have been on more or less the same alignment as the present road bridge, and the Roman road followed Bridge Street and Wood Street on its way westwards. There was probably a small roadside Roman settlement by the second century AD near the ford, but little is known about it.

Little or nothing more is known of what happened to that settlement after the Roman influence evaporated at the start of the fifth century AD. A pagan cemetery discovered in 1934 has been dated to the sixth century AD, and would suggest that there were still people living in the area during the so-called Dark Ages that followed. This part of modern-day Warwickshire became part of the early Saxon kingdom of the *Hwicce*, later a sub-kingdom of powerful Mercia. By AD 691, only a few years after a new Hwiccan diocese had been created based on a new cathedral at Worcester, there was a monastery at *Aet-Stretfordae*. This was most probably on or near the site of the present parish church, over half a mile from the ford. The diocese also owned large estates in the area, and while the monastery appears to have fallen victim to the Danish raids of the ninth and tenth centuries – and had certainly gone before the Norman conquest – the bishopric still held on to its property.

After the dramatic events of 1066, the Bishop of Worcester, Wulfstan, was one of the few Saxons allowed to keep his see and there was little local resistance to the new order. By the time the great Domesday Book was compiled, twenty years later, there was a small but prosperous settlement at *Stradforde,* seemingly little affected by the huge upheavals in national politics. This village had a population of around 200, a church, a water-mill and a fishery particularly noted for its eels – a thousand of which were sent to the bishop each year. Just over a century later, the whole picture was radically altered.

One thing that often puzzles, and sometimes exasperates or exhausts, pilgrims to Shakespeare's last resting place in Holy Trinity is the distance of the parish church from the centre of the town. The reason for this is hinted at in the name of that part of Stratford and of the road leading to it – Old Town. Towards the end of the twelfth century Stratford was still a small village clustered around its church. By this time the nearby Forest of Arden was gradually being cleared for farming and this created a need for new market centres in the region to deal with the growing amount of agricultural produce. In 1196 the bishop, John de Coutances, obtained a charter from the impoverished King Richard I for a weekly market at Stratford. Instead of simply expanding the old village, he ordered that a completely new town be laid out to the north. It was associated with a new wooden bridge that had been built across the Avon half a mile upstream from the old settlement to replace the ford on the old Roman road.

New towns are not just a twentieth-century idea. In the medieval period the creation of new towns served several different purposes. The most common function in a peaceful part of the country like Warwickshire was simply to bring in more money for the landowner, in this case the bishop. Those benefiting from living and working in the new town paid burgage rents for their properties, and those from the surrounding area selling their produce and wares in the market paid tolls. Provided there was a need for a new market

centre, the landowner could not fail to benefit from his enterprise.

The new borough was bound by the open fields belonging to the old settlement on three sides and by the river on the fourth. It consisted of three main streets running roughly parallel to the river, linked by three others running more or less at right angles to it. The arrangement is not quite the typical grid pattern of such medieval plantations, but more of a parallelogram with the shorter streets running at a slight angle to the longer ones. This was not a mistake, but an attempt to make maximum use of the slightly raised gravel terrace by the river and thus avoid the flood plain. The narrow strips of properties, called burgage plots, were laid out at right angles to the main streets. In Stratford, as in most new towns, their size was laid down by statute – in this case three and a half perches

3 Meer Street is a pleasantly curving street that once formed the northern boundary of the medieval marketplace, long infilled with buildings. It has a variety of pleasant if undistinguished buildings, and even the curving shopping range of 1956 blends in

wide and twelve perches long, an area of just over a quarter of an acre.

The old parish church was left outside the new settlement and for centuries there was to be sporadic friction between the old village, *Stratford Vetus*, and the new and separately administered borough, *Stratford Burgus*. One common cause of disharmony was the fact that the townspeople were denied their own chapel and had, technically, to worship in the parish church. It was not until 1610 that the new borough incorporated most of the Old Town.

The bishop's new town was a success. By 1251 there were 240 occupied burgages, over 50 other properties, and several shopkeepers and stallholders all paying rent. There were three separate marketplaces and listed among the inhabitants were clergymen, smiths, carpenters, wheelwrights, coopers, tilers, tanners, shoemakers, glovemakers, weavers, tailors, dyers, cooks and bakers. There was also a physician, a bridge-keeper, a piper and a minstrel. In the Old Town there were three corn mills and a fulling mill on the Avon, the latter being used to hammer and stretch cloth for Stratford's growing textile industry. All in all, the population had shot up to around 1,500 in just half a century.

The dislocation of town and church may have helped to make Stratford's guilds more powerful than they would normally have been. Guilds evolved as part-religious and part-lay self-help groups, dedicated to the upkeep of altars in churches and to helping the poor. There were at least three in Stratford by the late thirteenth century, but the Gild of the Holy Cross soon emerged as the most powerful. It was given large grants of land and the rents from these allowed it, effectively, to control civic life until the mid-sixteenth century. During this period, Stratford seems to have had a prosperous and fairly untroubled existence, partly because of the protection of its bishop. The town seldom got involved with national politics, even though occasionally one of its inhabitants would rise to high office. In the early fourteenth century, three of its rectors became chancellors of England. One, William Grenefield, went on to become Archbishop of York and another, John de Stratford, became Archbishop of Canterbury in 1333. Ralph de Stratford became Bishop of London in 1340, and in 1353, the

4 At the bottom end of the road, near to Waterside, is Nos. 30–31 Sheep Street, presently called Cordelia's, after the tragic but loyal daughter of King Lear. Built of close-studded timber-framing it is claimed to have been built in 1485, a time when Stratford was prospering

year before he died, he endowed a college for chantry priests in his home town near the church.

The town suffered, along with the rest of the country, in the mid-fourteenth century because of the effects of the Black Death, which wiped out anything between one-third and half of the population of England. Towards the end of the following century the town benefited from the generosity of another man of some stature, though no cleric – Sir Hugh Clopton. A native of Stratford, he made his money as a mercer in London, and was lord mayor of the capital in 1492. According to Leland he 'having never wife nor children convertid a greate peace of his substance in good works in Stratford'. This included building the stone bridge that still bears his name.

The Reformation had a typically muted affect on the town. True the guilds and the college for chantry priests were suppressed in 1547, but by 1553 much of their property and

5 Nos. 17–18 High Street form part of a fine row of early seventeenth-century houses and was apparently built in 1614. This view shows just how much timber there was in such buildings, and how easy it must have been for fire to spread rapidly. Like most buildings in Stratford it was stuccoed and rewindowed in the Georgian period, until being restored in 1920

6 The restoration of Shakespeare's Birthplace in the mid-nineteenth century was based largely on this engraving of 1769, published in the *Gentleman's Magazine*. This, in turn, was copied from a slightly earlier drawing

power had been given to a new corporation. Local government carried on more or less as it had done beforehand, with only the names of the officials being altered. By the time Shakespeare was born a few years later, Stratford was a fairly typical thriving Midland market town, with a population approaching 2,000. However, things were about to change again. Shortly after his birth the plague broke out and killed about 240 people. A recession in the wool trade towards the end of the century hit the town hard, and in 1590 it was said that Stratford had 'now fallen much in decay for want of such trade as heretofore . . . [it] . . . had by clothinge and makeinge of yarne'.

Much worse was to follow. On 22 September 1594, after a dry summer, a fire broke out and quickly devoured most of the timber-framed houses in High Street, Chapel Street, Wood Street and parts of Henley Street. Almost exactly a year later another fire destroyed houses between Sheep Street and Bridge Street. In all, an estimated 200 houses and countless outbuildings were lost, at an approximate cost of £20,000, then a huge amount. After the town had just got over this double disaster, yet another fire broke out in 1612 and 'within the space of lesse than two howers consumed and burnt fifty and fower dwelling-houses, many of them being very faire'. By this time the town's ability to recover had been seriously impaired and for well over 200 years it was in the economic doldrums.

At the start of the Civil War Stratford was undefended, in decline, and suffering from the effects of yet another fire in 1641 that had destroyed much of Bridge Street. It had no real strategic value to either side, apart from its bridge. By early 1643 this was of some importance to the Royalists, being the point where the route between their vital strongholds of Oxford and Shrewsbury crossed the road from Gloucester to Coventry. An attempt was made by Royalist troops from Oxfordshire under Colonel Wagstaffe to garrison the town. On 25 February his small force was routed at Welcombe Hill, just to the north, by Lord Brooke's parliamentary soldiers; Brooke went on to take the town. Shortly afterwards, three barrels of gunpowder stored in the new Town Hall blew up, more likely because of an accidental spark than Royalist derring-do. The building was virtually destroyed in the blast and other buildings nearby badly damaged. The town never again figured prominently in the war, but still had enough problems of its own to deal with when the plague broke out again in 1645 and took over sixty lives.

Economic gloom continued in Stratford after the Restoration in 1660, despite ambitious plans to improve matters. Shortly before the war William Sandys had obtained an Act that would allow him to form a company to make 'the River of Avon passible for bringinge of wares from sondrye places to this borough of Stratford'. It is unclear how much of the work was finished when hostilities commenced, but in 1667 another engineer, Andrew Yarranton, had started to repair the locks on the navigation. He also came up with a rather amazing scheme to revitalize the town. He planned to create another two new towns just outside the Bishop of Worcester's medieval one. One, at Milcot, was to be called New Harlem and have a population of 10,000 producing thread. The other, just over the Clopton

ANN HATHAWAY'S COTTAGE
STRATFORD-ON-AVON.

7 By the time this postcard of Anne Hathaway's Cottage was sent in the early years of this century, Stratford-upon-Avon was well and truly on the tourist map and the 'Shakespeare industry' was thriving

bridge, was to be called New Brunswick and produce German-style beer! Nothing came of the towns but Yarranton at least finished the navigation that Daniel Defoe described in the 1720s as 'an exceeding advantage to all this part of the country'. All sorts of luxuries and necessities were imported from Bristol, including wine, sugar, lead and iron, with the main products sent down river being cheese and corn.

The erratic economic recovery faltered again in the mid-eighteenth century but in the 1760s a chain of events began that would, eventually, establish the town's most famous industry. The war damage to the Town Hall had been patched up in 1661, but a century later the building was in a very poor state of repair and a new one was desperately needed. Raising the money, not surprisingly, proved hard, but then someone in the Corporation had a bright idea. One of the leading lights in the revival of Shakespearian drama in the eighteenth century was the actor David Garrick. His ego was known to be as great as his acting talents, and he was approached by the Corporation

to give money to help the Bard's home town, and to add to his own reputation in the process. Garrick readily agreed, but what was to be a fairly simple donation of money ended up as a full-blown celebration of Shakespeare in 1769. It lasted for three days, and brought the prime of London society to what was then a provincial backwater. A temporary timber amphitheatre or Rotunda was built and parades and speeches were organized. Even though the event was dogged by torrential rain, lack of adequate accommodation and poor organization, Shakespeare's home town had been put well and truly on the fashionable map.

Immediately afterwards there was no huge surge of visitors, partly because there was little else to do in the town apart from visiting Shakespeare's Birthplace and partly because of the general problems of transport in Georgian England. The American writer Washington Irving was typical of the more

8 The splendid Swan's Nest Hotel at the south end of the bridge was built around 1673 for John Clopton. It was probably part of the ambitious plans of Yarranton to develop this area and is a rare early example of brick-build in Stratford. It has had an eventful life, being the Bear Inn, then a warehouse, and then the Shoulder of Mutton

9 The view across the Avon to the Royal Shakespeare Theatre has become a much photographed one since Elisabeth Scott's competition-winning design opened in 1932. From this angle the trees and landscaped grounds and the lively riverside balconies soften its ungainly utilitarianism. From other sides it is just bleak and boring. Inside, however, as a theatre, it works

adventurous type of tourist in 1815 when he was shown around the

> squalid chambers . . . [of the] . . . small mean-looking
> edifice of wood and plaster . . . by a garrulous old lady in a
> frosty red face, lighted up by a cold blue anxious eye, and
> garnished with artificial locks of flaxen hair, curling from
> under an exceedingly dirty cap.

The town itself was at last beginning to revive in the early nineteenth century, in part because of improvements in transport. The local roads were turnpiked at the end of the eighteenth century, the canal was opened in 1816 and the Stratford & Moreton Tramway in 1826. New mills had been built by the weir and in 1831 Edward Flower founded the brewery firm that would eventually become one of the town's chief employers. The population of the borough, which had been more or less static since the end of the sixteenth century, rose from 2,418 in 1801 to 3,672 in 1861 and continued to rise gradually.

The development of the national railway network in the 1840s would clearly boost the number of visitors to the town, and the potential profits to be made from Shakespeare's Birthplace were seen by its owner. In 1806 it had been sold for just £210, and no mention had been made of its claim to fame. In 1847 it was bought at auction for the then-staggering sum of £3,000. Fortunately, the purchasers were members of a new trust set up specifically to preserve the building and to encourage Shakespearian study. The Shakespeare Birthplace Trust has been doing exactly that ever since, owns many other properties associated with Shakespeare, has a superb archive, and an academic reputation renowned the world over.

Today Stratford is a very busy town of about 20,000 permanent inhabitants, but usually bulging with many thousands more all the year round. Its streets are crammed with tourists and its air full of dozens of different languages. On a more homely scale it is still a very popular day-out destination for people from the nearby urban conurbations, an inland resort with attractive riverside parks and the irresistible

10 The Garrick, in the High Street, has cusped braces in its square-panelled, jettied upper floors and decorative bargeboards in the two gables, which is unusual for Stratford. It has been an inn since at least the start of the eighteenth century and has had several names, including the Reindeer and the Greyhound. The present name commemorates the famous actor, who put the town back on the map

11 A typical carpenter's mark cut into a timber of the Shakespeare Hotel. It is probably an 8 – in Roman numerals – but the extra line in the 'V' and the gouged curve in the last 'I' would have meant something to the builders

opportunity to go 'messing about on the river'. It is a major cultural centre, of course, with the Memorial Theatre and its satellites putting on some of the finest productions in the world – contemporary and avant-garde as well as Shakespearian and period. Beneath all this there is still the important market town and commercial centre, carrying on the same basic functions that the bishop's new town was laid out for at the end of the twelfth century.

Architectural Character

In the 1540s Leland wrote that Stratford had 'two or three very lardge stretes, besydes bake lanes' and was 'reasonbly well buyldyd of tymber'. More than four hundred years later the character of central Stratford has, in many ways, changed remarkably little. The rigid medieval street plan of the bishop's new town survives intact, although the huge triangular marketplace once bounded by Henley, Wood and Meer streets has long been covered by buildings. Temporary market trestles gradually gave way to market stalls that it turn gave way to buildings, the owners of which paid annual fines for the privilege. This process of 'market infilling' happened in most towns, often resulting in narrow streets and cramped building plots. In Stratford it was well under way as early as the fourteenth century, and there was also similar infilling on Bridge Street. However, the dilapidated row of timber-framed houses running down the middle of Bridge Street – aptly named Middle Row – was swept away in the nineteenth century.

Stratford's wide streets allow its historic buildings to be seen to good advantage, a fact noted by a writer in the 1820s who considered the place 'small but handsome and airy . . . [and] . . . much more regular in its plan and buildings than the generality of towns of any antiquity'. He went on to say that it contained 'many old houses, presenting curious specimens of early domestic architecture'. Far more of these 'specimens' are now exposed to the public gaze than would have been the case then, but many are still hidden behind later façades and finishes. All

12 The doorcase of Old Town Place is a rather fine one, though slightly unusual; it dates to the early eighteenth century

13 This splendid Tudor Gothic Revival doorway belongs to No. 17 Old Town, part of a curving terrace built in 1842

14 Although this door and doorway to the Shakespeare Hotel are of some antiquity, neither are in their original places. Note how the moulding of the lintel stops well short of the right-hand side of the present door opening

15 The quality of the gauged brick arches framing this doorcase, to No. 23 Birmingham Road, is superb – particulary in the 'ogee' arch over the door itself. This is late Georgian work, possibly from the early decades of the nineteenth century

16 An early eighteenth-century window of Trinity College, Church Street, with fine gauged brick head enriched with a stone keystone. The thin glazing bars are much later

17 Until the end of the seventeenth century, most windows in the more up-to-date houses would still have been casements – like this cross-mullioned example of about 1702 in the Old Vicarage, part of the grammar school

have had to adapt over the centuries to changing needs and fashions.

Until the eighteenth century, Stratford was still very much a timber-framed town. The local stone is a very poor material for building and was usually confined to the low plinths on which the timber-framed houses stand, or to the occasional chimney stack. The only stone buildings of note – Holy Trinity and the Gild chapel – were built of stone brought in from outside the town. It was considered essential that such important structures were built in material of the highest status, which is also why the long-lost college in Old Town was also built of stone.

18 These Gothick windows of 1768 in Church Street are surrounded by early nineteenth-century render, and have been tacked on to a timber-framed building of 1600!

19 A typical three-light casement window with diamond-patterned 'quarries' in the Falcon, Chapel Street. This particular window is clearly a modern copy – but a good one

The most obvious materials to build with in this part of Warwickshire could be found in the Forest of Arden. Timber, especially English oak, was in abundance, and the construction of timber-framed buildings the logical outcome. The felled trees were normally cut, sawn and measured in the carpenter's yard and the pieces of the individual frames slotted together temporarily on the yard floor. Individual joins between timbers were then numbered, usually in a series of debased Roman numerals gouged or scratched into the wood. The frames were dismantled, and the timbers carted to the building site to be re-erected. The numbers, or carpenter's marks, made sure, if all went well, that everything went back in the right order, and they can often still be seen on exposed timbers even hundreds of years later.

20 One of the elaborately carved door-heads of the Almshouses in Church Street

21 This fine hound, decorating a bracket of Harvard House, is probably a Talbot

22 No. 18 Greenhill Street is a small, close-studded, timber-framed house probably dating to the early sixteenth century. It is of a type that would have been built in great numbers away from the more expensive central part of the town

23 Despite being swallowed up by Stratford, much of Shottery has retained the rural character of the early seventeenth century, as in this lovely row of cottages

All the surviving timber-framed buildings in Stratford are of box-frame construction, and often jettied. The overhanging, or jettying, out of one or more of the upper floors on one or more sides is common but was not, as is often thought, done simply to increase floor space. It helped to make the upper floors more stable because of the weight distribution of the jettied frames, and meant that shorter posts could be used. Jetties tended to be quite wide in the medieval period, but they got shallower and shallower towards the end of the sixteenth century and eventually became virtually decorative.

One distinct characteristic of Stratford's timber-framed buildings is the use of close-studding. The cheapest way to build in timber was to have square or rectangular panels,

24 No. 30 High Street was restored in 1918, at which point its fine timber frame was uncovered. The two original gables with their finely carved tie-beams lost their tops when the space between them was infilled to create a second storey. The building probably dates to around 1600

infilled with 'wattle-and-daub'. Generally, staves were fitted into a series of drilled holes in the underside of the upper rail of the panel and then sprung into a long groove cut into the top of the lower rail. Pliable branches were then woven between the staves to complete the key (the wattle) for the daub, an often horrendous mixture of clay, animal hair and dung. Once dry, this was covered by a thin plaster skin.

In close-studded frames, vertical posts, or studs, were placed very close together, usually only as far apart as they were wide. Short split laths were clipped into grooves in the sides of the studs to act as the key for the plastered daub infilling. Close-studding obviously used up a tremendous amount of timber and was structurally unnecessary. Nevertheless, from the start of the fifteenth century, and possibly from sometime before that, the builders of Stratford clearly delighted in using

25 The aptly named Shakespeare Hotel has a magnificent 120-foot-long façade. The longer southern section was rebuilt soon after the 1594 fire, but the northern portion is considered to be slightly older. This section was damaged when the Town Hall blew up in the Civil War, then given a brick façade. It was rebuilt again in 1920 by the Justins family as a memorial to the local dead of the First World War. The same family had restored the other section in 1882

26 At the back of many Stratford houses, including, for example, that of John Shakespeare on Henley Street, were rows of timber-framed stores and workshops built around yards. Such a building is this one, built behind a Henley Street house but now reached from Guild Street. It probably dates to around 1600 and its latest restoration in 1986 won an award, even though some of the alterations have not respected the original design

close-studded and jettied frames. Early examples include the Guildhall and the Almshouses in Church Street, and Alveston Manor over the river in Bridgetown. This profligate use of timber continued even up until the start of the seventeenth century, by which time wood had become a relatively scarce commodity and restrictions had been placed on its use to protect stocks. The only obvious difference between the medieval and post-medieval close-studding is the gradual introduction of a mid-rail by the latter part of the sixteenth century – and the general increase in height of the buildings. The earlier ones tended to be of just two storeys, the later ones of three.

As a whole Warwickshire, unlike the western Midland counties, never really had a strong tradition of ornately carved

27 Thatch was once a common roof covering in Stratford, but here, as elsewhere, its use was blamed for the fires that periodically ravaged timber-framed towns. The Old Thatch Tavern on Greenhill Street is the only building in the centre of town to have a thatched roof today

28 Early brickwork is rare in Stratford, which makes what has been done to No. 5 Chapel Street that much worse. Behind the horrid ground-floor extensions is a fine brick front dating from 1673. Articulated with vaguely Doric pilasters, it would make a superb contribution to the streetscape were it restored

and decorated timber-frames. Harvard House in the High Street is very much the exception to this rule in Stratford. There are a few examples of diamond pattern bracing in some of the late sixteenth-century timber-frames, but in general the framing is very simple and workmanlike, despite the obvious cost in timber. One notable feature of the later buildings built towards the end of the sixteenth century is the use of very large windows, often flanked by smaller windows high in the framing – sometimes called frieze windows.

It is, incidentally, important to remember that these timber-framed buildings were never designed to be painted black and white. Originally, the oak would have been allowed to retain its own colour and age naturally. Some of the panel infills were painted, but not usually just in white. The 'tradition' of black timbers came about partly because of the use of pitch and tar

29 This house on Windsor Street is a good example of how timber-framed buildings, in this case probably dating from the early seventeenth century, were often refronted in brick in the eighteenth century. The framing is still visible in the gable wall

preservative on what were then old and rotting timbers from the later eighteenth century onwards – the look caught on because of the general misunderstanding of exactly what had happened. The result today is a conservationist dilemma. When timber-framed buildings are being restored, should they be restored to their original state – if known – or to the 'black-and-white' so beloved of the guide books and tourists. There are no easy answers.

One building material once common to Stratford is now virtually extinct in the town centre, but can be seen in Shottery. Picturesque thatched 'black-and-white' cottages in sleepy hamlets conjure up 'olde Englande' for many people, and

30 The date plaque of No. 5 Chapel Street

31 The brick-facing process is less easy to see in this plain-looking building, Nos. 41–42 Henley Street. The brick front probably dates from the early nineteenth century, but the recently restored interior is a real surprise

32 Concealed behind the façade of Nos. 41–42 Henley Street is an almost intact late fifteenth-century timber-framed house complete with the remains of a galleried hall and cross-wing. In these photographs the arch-headed front door helps to link the internal and external views

33 Croft School in Old Town looks to be of early eighteenth century date, possibly from the 1720s. Originally consisting of the five symmetrical bays to the right, it is one of the better Georgian town houses in Stratford. The bays to the left are part of an extension. The join between the two is difficult to spot, but can be seen in the cornice, for example

anyone visiting Anne Hathaway's will not be disappointed. However, in towns, the use of thatch on the roofs of tightly grouped rows of timber-framed houses dramatically increased the already high risk of fire. The conflagrations that consumed large areas of Stratford at the end of the sixteenth century were said to have 'had their beginnings in poore Tenements and Cottages wch were thatched with strawe', despite an edict of 1583 forbidding its use. Even after the first two fires, a survey in 1599 showed that although buildings lining the streets were mainly tiled, the back buildings were still often thatched. The Corporation were so concerned about the lax way in which their edicts were being obeyed that they persuaded the Privy Council to support their by-laws. The aptly named Old Thatch Tavern on Greenhill Street is now the only thatched house in the centre of the town, although many other buildings,

including the Gild's Almshouses in Church Street, used to be. It is interesting to note that the more important Guildhall next door was roofed with a material considered then to be of higher status – clay tiles.

The area around Stratford had a well-established tile industry at this time, and the allied skills of brickmaking using the local clays were also known. So it is perhaps somewhat surprising that there is so little evidence of the early use of brick in the town. The Great House built in the late fifteenth century by Hugh Clopton in Chapel Street was 'a praty howse of brike and tymber', but despite the risk of fires the buildings constructed after the two great fires of the 1590s were all rebuilt in timber-framing – not brick. For most people the new material was too expensive to build in, and for the wealthy it possibly also lacked the potential ostentation of timber-framing. Apart from these considerations, there were simply

34 The chequer pattern brick so popular in Stratford in the first half of the nineteenth century can be seen in this pair of semi-detached town houses in Rother Street. Now Warwickshire County Council offices, they probably date from the very end of the eighteenth century, or early in the nineteenth

35 The Red Lion in Bridge Foot was first licensed in 1821 but is clearly a much older building, dating back to the previous century at least. It was renovated in 1984–5

36 Now marooned on a traffic island, this delightful little early eighteenth-century summer-house once stood in the gardens of nearby Alveston Manor

too few architects and craftsmen with the necessary skills to
build in brick. At least by this time most chimneys had to be
built in brick, by law – before, many had been timber-framed.

In the second half of the seventeenth century, a period when
brick was much more widely accepted and, indeed, was
becoming the only fashionable material to build in, Stratford
was not a prosperous place. Nevertheless, it can still boast two
early brick buildings of note, both dating to the early 1670s
and both, no doubt, influenced by the use of brick in the
remodelling just beforehand of Clopton House, a mile or so out
of the town. The larger of the two in Stratford itself is now the
Swan's Nest Hotel in Bridgefoot, just across the Clopton
Bridge. It may have had some connection with Yarranton's
abortive New Brunswick scheme, and was built of bricks made
on site. The other, No. 5 Chapel Street, can often be missed

because of the rather horrible modern extensions at ground-floor level. The brick façade is pilastered and bears the date 1673 and the initials 'CEA', possibly a reference to Edward and Alice Canning.

Throughout the eighteenth century towns and cities across England were being rebuilt in brick. In the more prosperous, the timber-framed buildings would be swept away completely and replaced. Sometimes, if the money was not available, just the fronts would be faced with brick. At the very least, the frames would be covered with lath and plaster to try and keep up with the latest architectural fashion for symmetry and simplicity. In poverty-stricken Stratford, this last option was

38 Neo-Elizabethan decoration was popular in Stratford in the early nineteenth century, as shown in this pleasantly curving terrace of 1842 on the corner of Old Town. The ornate barge boards owe little to historical research but add a suitable finishing touch. Note, too, the typical Stratford chequer brickwork

the one most often followed, although the town does have a reasonable collection of good-quality early eighteenth-century brick buildings, particularly in the Old Town area. There are fewer examples of the middle Georgian period, when the town was in decline again, and no large-scale developments of the fashionable terraces, crescents or squares then popular in more successful towns and cities.

Only in the early nineteenth century did brick begin to dominate the appearance of the town, and even then it was often used simply to replace decayed wattle-and-daub panel infills in the ancient timber-frames. This use of brick is called brick-nogging. Other buildings were built or faced with better-quality brick fronts. Ironically, this was also the same time that the architectural fashion called for the covering up of

40 The various antique architectural styles used in the early nineteenth century were only used as motifs to decorate otherwise purely standard late Georgian buildings. This pair of neo-Elizabethan houses on the Warwick Road is typical. The houses have stuccoed brickwork, dripstones over the ornately glazed casements, and rather half-hearted gables breaking up the roof line. They probably date to the 1830s or 1840s and may well have been designed by the architect who was responsible for the spa buildings at Bishopton

brickwork with Roman Cement – or stucco – lined to imitate high-quality ashlar. Stratford has several examples of stuccoed façades of this period and the revival of the town's economic fortunes is mirrored in its architecture.

One interesting brick technique that became popular in the town was the use of the chequer pattern. Most of the locally hand-made Georgian and early Victorian facing brick used has a fairly gentle red colour. Around the sides and backs of buildings, and in internal walls, the common or 'place' bricks were much paler and of inferior quality. The usual way of putting bricks together, the 'bond', was the 'Flemish'. This is characterized on the outside of the wall by alternating 'stretchers' – that is, the long sides of the bricks – and 'headers' – their ends – in each course. By using the better red facing bricks as stretchers and the paler bricks as headers, a

42 Albany Road was mainly laid out in the early years of this century and these attractive roughcast semis were designed by John Brearley in 1911

quite pleasing chequer pattern emerges. From old photographs, it looks as if part of Shakespeare's Birthplace was faced with this type of brickwork early in the nineteenth century, and it was used in both humble artisan terraces and quite grand houses.

In the early nineteenth century architectural fashion veered away from correctness and classic proportions towards the picturesque antique, with a proliferation of styles derived from what had gone before – neo-Tudor, neo-Elizabethan and neo-Gothic to name just three – often used indiscriminately. Stratford even has, in Brewery Street, a unique pair of semi-detached houses whose details can only be described as neo-Saxon. Their triangular window heads were meant, presumably, to copy those of Saxon churches such as

43 In Bridge Street the polished black and somewhat brutal façade of this shop comes as a shock. It was built in 1933, in the then very up-to-date house style of Burton's, the tailors

Deerhurst. This interest in the architectural styles of the past inevitably resulted in more attention being paid to the genuine historic buildings that had survived the ravages of time. In the late nineteenth century, thousands of old houses throughout England were 'restored' as acres of stucco and brick were cleared away to expose the hidden timber frames behind. The results varied from the sympathetic and acceptable to the ruthless and radical.

In general, the buildings in Stratford were relatively well looked after and a considerable amount of thought seems to have gone into how they should be restored. The earliest and most famous restoration was, of course, that of Shakespeare's Birthplace. The new Trust's initial action would make modern conservationists cringe. They bought the row of timber-framed buildings on either side of the house – and promptly knocked them all down! The rationale for this apparent act of vandalism was to remove all possibility of fire spreading to the Birthplace. The Birthplace itself was in a very poor state

of repair and part of it, which had been a public house – the Swan and Maidenhead – since Shakespeare's time, was faced in brick. The Trust wanted to restore it to its sixteenth-century state, but for the Henley Street façade they had only some limited structural evidence and an engraving of 1769 taken in turn from an earlier drawing. The restoration was based on the engraving, which was clearly flawed in some of its details; the pattern of timbers in the dormers is most unusual, for example.

Nevertheless, the way in which the main restoration was carried out, in 1860–61, was exemplary for its time and a part of the architect's specifications are well worth quoting:

The builder was to remove all those excrescences which are decidedly the result of modern innovation, to uphold with jealous care all that now exists of undoubted

44 It is not very often that 1950s' buildings are worthy of praise, but this 1953 development in Greenhill Street is an exception. It does what every good urban building should do: it fits in with the existing streetscape while still being a positive architectural statement. Its huge pitched roof has a hint of the medieval, and the revival of the jetty has the practical purpose of providing shelter for anyone entering the deliberately offset shopfronts below

antiquity, not to destroy any portion about whose character the slightest doubt does now exist, but to restore any parts needing it in such manner that the restoration can never be mistaken for the old work though harmonizing with it.

This philosophy of repair for a vernacular building was way ahead of its time. Indeed, this approach is the one that is officially accepted today, although it was well over a hundred years before it was taken as seriously as it should have been. Remove the Shakespeare legend from the Birthplace and it becomes a pleasant but apparently insignificant timber-framed building. Yet it is one that can, quite fairly, be considered an important landmark in the history of architectural conservation.

The Birthplace Trust would, over the following decades, acquire other houses connected with Shakespeare and restore them in the same manner. Also active in sympathetic restorations was Charles Flower, the brewer, and a patron of

46 The former Stratford Hilton, now the Moat House, built at the start of the 1970s, did not even attempt to fit in with the town's character. Long and at least low, its rubblestone-clad ground floor walling is simply ridiculous

many good local causes including the first Memorial Theatre. It was he that paid for the restoration of the medieval Almshouses in Church Street in 1892. Shortly afterwards another famous author came to live in Stratford – the eccentric Marie Corelli. Fame, for her at least, was fleeting. As a writer of romantic novels she considered herself almost as Shakespeare's equal, and clearly thought the town was lucky to have a second literary genius. She set herself up as a guardian of its heritage. To her credit, she was involved in the restoration work on the Library in Henley Street, as well as that of the Garrick and Harvard House in the High Street. Often the old timber frames needed very radical rebuilding, and there is sometimes very little of the original work left. The restoration of old timber-framed buildings, in Stratford and

47 This row of timber-framed cottages, Nos. 30–34 Ely Street, are thought to date to the late sixteenth century, but could easily have been built a century later. They were virtually rebuilt in 1971

elsewhere, lcd to an inevitable vogue for building new ones, and the town has a few pretty awful examples.

In many way, Stratford has never, architecturally, come to terms with the twentieth century. There are a few reasonably good examples of uncompromisingly modern buildings of the 1930s and 1950s, but, with the notable exception of the Shakespeare Centre, the ones built from the 1960s onwards have been less than successful. The early 1960s Post Office in Bridge Street is an unmitigated planning disaster; Sir Frederick Gibberd's 1959–64 development of the old Corn Exchange site at the corner of Sheep Street and High Street was much praised at the time and won a Civic Trust award, but now looks naïve and dated; and the Moat House Hotel near the river, built in the early 1970s as the Stratford Hilton, is just far too boring, and far too big.

Since the 1970s, architects in Stratford, under pressure from public opinion and from developers, have retreated from modernism to post-modernism and what can only be described as the pseudo-vernacular style. In many respects it is difficult to judge these buildings fairly in the early 1990s, but some judgement has to be made. It is not in the main an enthusiastic one. Well treated, using the right materials and the right proportions for buildings in the right place, it can work reasonably well. The main problem in Stratford is that many of the developments are too ambitious for their own good. Debased varieties of traditional styles imported from all over the country have been grafted on to otherwise identical buildings; plastic timber-framing has made its unwelcome appearance on four- or five-storey 'vernacular' blocks; and the perfectly good buildings in the former Flower's Brewery off Birmingham Road have been demolished and replaced by new apartments, designed to look like perfectly good brewery buildings. Pastiche is everywhere, not an honest bit of architecture in sight. By and large the centre is safe, but the pressure on the planners for more residential accommodation in such a popular town is enormous, and the solutions enormously hard to find.

Churches

Holy Trinity parish church, seen across the steadily flowing and tree-flanked Avon, is one of the timeless views of England, and one of the best known. There has probably been a church here for a thousand years or more, for although no remains of the Saxon monastery at Stratford have yet been found it is generally believed to have been on or near this site. It was probably little more than a collection of timber-framed buildings with its own small timber-framed chapel.

Nothing obvious survives from the church that stood here in 1086, even though that may have been built of stone. The earliest surviving parts of the present building appear to belong to the mid-thirteenth century. This early church seems to have been cruciform in plan, with aisled nave and chancel and transepts, built in the first true native Gothic style, the Early English. This is typified by the tall lancet windows in the present transepts, which have survived the many subsequent changes to the fabric.

In the early fourteenth century a major remodelling took place that included altering and raising the crossing tower, giving it the fine round 'rose' windows in the process. Both nave aisles date from this period, the north one probably being widened and the south one completely built anew. All this work, in the aptly named Decorated style, is generally attributed to John de Stratford, Archbishop of Canterbury. The stonework is fairly rough-coursed rubble that is now badly eroded – grey stone for the bulk of the walls and a brighter, beige-yellow ashlared stone for the decorative features around openings and for the quoins. No doubt originally the latter stone could be more easily worked and moulded, but it has worn as badly as, if not worse than, the grey.

In the 1480s the old chancel was pulled down and replaced by a fine new one on the orders of Dean Thomas Balshall. This time the masonry was of far superior quality. A grey stone, presumably imported from quarries not too distant, was used. It could be easily worked and 'ashlared' – that is, worked to a smooth finish and lain in regular courses. It contrasts remarkably with the older masonry. The style chosen was the one in fashion at the time – the last of the true native Gothic styles, the Perpendicular. As its much later name suggests, there was a definite stress on height and verticality, and, as well, a tremendous emphasis on light and on the use of larger and larger windows. Many find the end result a little mechanical, but the skill of the masons has to be admired. The huge windows in this superb portion of Holy Trinity are typical of the period, five in each side wall and a magnificent east window occupying virtually all of that end of the church; it is one of the best examples of its type and date in England.

Yet more light was soon flooding in through an unusually tall clerestory added, shortly after Balshall's death in 1491, by his successor, Dean Collingwood. It is virtually a continuous row of windows on either side, with very narrow masonry piers in between them. Again a better quality of ashlared stone was used, probably from the same quarry, and it seems clear that the great west window, restored in 1950, was added at the same time. The door and the masonry below it belong to an earlier period. The north porch was also added during this rebuilding work, and its east wall cuts clumsily into one of the windows in the north aisle.

Of this general phase too is the remodelling of what became known as the Clopton chapel, now containing the much-restored tomb of Hugh Clopton – the man who had probably paid for much of the work on the church and who so benefited the town up until his death in 1496. The master mason involved with all this work may have been Thomas Dowland, who was also responsible for the rebuilding of the Gild chapel in the same style and during the same period.

At about the same time, a skilled carpenter was carving the mischievous misericords in the chancel, medieval life captured in miniature. Misericords are drop-down seats for the clerics and choristers in the stalls with projecting 'corbels' that

48 The church of Holy Trinity was in existence in the late Saxon period, but the earliest portions only date from the mid-thirteenth century, by which time a new Stratford was being developed to the south of the old village. This view is from the north-east, showing architectural phases of the thirteenth, fourteenth, fifteenth and eighteenth centuries

allowed them to appear to be standing up during the often intermidable medieval services while actually resting their backsides. They were often carved with a huge variety of topics, and the subject matter was not always that reverent, as in some of the ones in Holy Trinity.

Apart from the spire, the church looks little different today than when Leland described the recently remodelled edifice in around the 1540s as 'a fayre large peace of worke'. The wooden medieval spire that stood on top of the tower was just 42 feet high. Described as 'old mean . . . [and] . . . leaden', it had become dangerous by the mid-eighteenth century and was taken down in 1762. The present stone replacement was built in the following year by William Hiorne to a design by Thomas Lightoler. The only other major loss the church has suffered, and one not lamented by many, was a decaying charnel house attached to it, pulled down in 1800.

By the early nineteenth century the church was in a very poor state of repair. One writer was shocked that the church fortunate enough to contain 'the ashes of the most intellectual mortal that ever lived – should have been suffered to fall into decay, and even to be nearly threatened with demolition'. Three thousand pounds and more were spent in the restoration work started in 1835 under the supervision of the Worcester architect Harvey Eginton. Much of the money needed was raised through an exceedingly unpopular church rate. Although there was some general patching of the external masonry and internal plaster all over the church, the most important work was concentrated on the chancel. Dean Balshall's roof had been removed in the eighteenth century and been replaced by a plain flat one, so Eginton designed a brand new neo-Gothic oak roof. Just over fifty years later, between 1888 and 1892, the church was restored again, this time far more radically. The architects involved were George Frederick Bodley and Thomas Garner, one of the most respected partnerships of the day when it came to church architecture -- old or new – but often seen, from the safe assurance of retrospect, as being rather heavy-handed in their restoration work.

Of course, most people come not as admirers of the

49 The huge west window of Holy Trinity was built in the 1490s, but the doorway beneath is earlier, as is the south aisle to the nave. Beneath the battlements are the windows of the clerestory, added to the nave along with the west window. The spire that dominates the views of this part of the Avon valley was added as recently as 1763

50 The sanctuary knocker on the door of the north door of Holy Trinity

51 The mainly fifteenth-century Gild chapel is often mistaken for the parish church – it is, after all, in the middle of the town. Built by the powerful gilds as their own chapel and next to their Guildhall (just visible to the right), it also served as a chapel of ease for the town and so escaped demolition at the Dissolution

architectural delights of Holy Trinity but as pilgrims to stand near the last resting place of the Bard. He was buried in the chancel not because of his fame or fortune, but because it was his right as a local burgess. The famous alabaster wall monument and effigy on the north wall was carved by his friend Gerard Johnson. Hugh Clopton is also buried in the church, in his own chapel off the north aisle, and there are several other good monuments. Holy Trinity is undoubtedly one of the finest parish churches in the Midlands, and even if Shakespeare hadn't been buried here, it would still be well worth the long walk from the town centre to see it.

Considering just how far away from the middle of town Holy Trinity is, visitors to Stratford can be forgiven for thinking that the fine Gild chapel at the end of Chapel Street is the parish church, and it certainly looks the part. According to Leland it was Hugh Clopton that 'made in the middle of the towne a right fair and large chapelle' at the end of the fifteenth

52 The remains of a splendid painted 'Doom' over the chancel arch inside the Gild chapel are a reminder that such churches were not originally bare-walled. These paintings often covered all the available walls and acted as a picture book on the teachings of the church, with a particular emphasis on Hell and damnation

53 The Baptist chapel in Payton Street was built in 1835 and is a simple but dignified neo-classical structure with a Tuscan portico. To the right is the less-dignified Italianate school added in 1861; it has definite similarities with the railway station

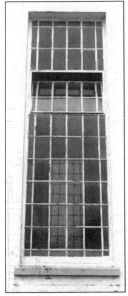

54 The side windows of the Payton Street Baptist chapel taper in towards an otherwise normal flat-arched window head. It must have caused the bricklayers tremendous trouble, but the design was presumably an attempt to suggest height

century. This is not quite true; he did indeed pay for it to be radically rebuilt, but the building had been started in 1269. In that year the newly combined Gild of the Holy Cross, the Blessed Virgin and St John the Baptist was sufficiently rich and powerful to persuade Bishop Giffard to let it build its own chapel, independent of the parish church. Little survives of the first chapel, and the oldest part of the present building seems to be the chancel, probably rebuilt in the 1420s and quite a simple and unpretentious structure.

Hugh Clopton paid the mason Thomas Dowland to rebuild the nave, north porch, and west tower in the 1490s, giving the building its battlemented late-Perpendicular appearance. The effect of the rebuilding was to make the nave the grandest part of the church – completely dominating the far humbler, but liturgically more important, chancel and even making the contemporary west tower look a little insignificant. The four huge windows in each side give the interior a feeling of light and height.

Over the arch to the chancel is a wall-painted 'Doom', seen by Leland but whitewashed soon afterwards as Reformation zeal took hold. The paintings were only rediscovered when the whitewash was stripped from the walls as the chapel was being extensively restored in 1804. The paintings were consolidated earlier this century, and others are now hidden, and protected, behind modern panelling on the side walls. These frescos, now very faded, would once have been vibrant with colour – perhaps far too vibrant for modern sensibilities. They were tremendously important aids in teaching the Christian faith in medieval times when virtually the entire congregation was illiterate and the Bible was in Latin. Unfortunately they were considered blasphemous when Protestantism swept through England and were usually destroyed or painted over.

Matters could have been worse in Stratford. The Gild chapel itself was threatened with demolition after the Gild was disbanded in 1547 as part of the general process of reform. The much-feared Royal Commissioners were sent out into the country by Henry VIII and by the men that controlled his successor, the boy king Edward VI, to loot Church property. However, after their visit to Stratford they reported that it was 'very mete and necessary that the Gild Chapel of Stratford stand undefaced for that it was always a chapell of ease . . . and standith in the face of the towne'.

The Gild chapel remained a semi-official chapel-of-ease for centuries and it was only in 1855 that a new church was opened in the new borough – St James's, in Guild Street. This was an uninspired neo-Gothic affair designed by a little-known architect, James Murray, and it was not a great architectural loss to the town when it was pulled down in the 1950s.

Nonconformity has had a long history in Stratford but has left only one building of any architectural merit. The Baptist chapel in the late Georgian development of Payton Street was opened in 1835 and financed largely by James Cox, a timber merchant. With its Tuscan-columned portico it is an extremely simple and chaste neoclassical design, built just as the Gothic Revival in church architecture was beginning to sweep all before it. The tapering windows in the side walls are of particular interest. At the moment, even the rather odd shade of

55 The religious revival in the Victorian period corresponded with a renewed fascination in death and the afterlife. Old churchyards could no longer cope with burials, so municipal cemeteries were laid out in the outskirts. Stratford has a particularly fine and well-kept late nineteenth-century example. Its vaguely French Gothic mortuary chapel has been opened up as a shelter for visitors

flaking pale green paint cannot take much away from the essential dignity of the building.

The rather inept Wesleyan chapel of 1835 on the Birmingham Road and the uninspiring polychrome brick Primitive Methodist chapel of 1866 in Great William Street were both designed in an insipid Italianate style, and both are closed. A modern Methodist chapel and hall has been built in brick and stone-cladding opposite the west end of Holy Trinity. Its only notable architectural feature is its modern, open, spire. At least the former Congregational church in Rother Street is still in use, now as a United Reformed church. Built to the

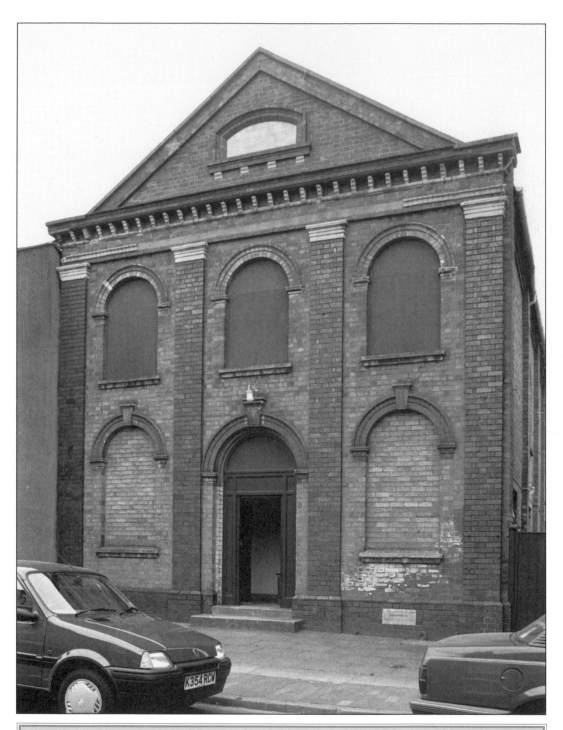

56 Redundant chapels, and indeed churches, are a conservationist's nightmare. What can be done with them? The former Primitive Methodist chapel on Great William Street of 1866 was built of imported brick in the vague Italianate style often chosen for Nonconformist chapels. It is of little architectural merit, but is an accepted part of the streetscape

57 St Gregory's Roman Catholic church stands on the Warwick Road next to the manse, which was probably built at the same time. The architect was Edward Pugin, son of the more famous Augustus Welby Pugin, a key figure in the Gothic Revival. This particular example, opened in 1866, is not one of the best

designs of H.J. Paul and opened in 1880, it is certainly not one of the better essays in neo-Gothic Nonconformist places of worship. Its appearance has not been helped by the loss of its miniature spire. The inside is of a little more interest, however, with good decoration, furnishings, and cast-iron piers.

Roman Catholics were gradually given more freedom to worship in the early nineteenth century after suffering the best part of three centuries of persecution. The first Stratford congregation had a temporary chapel in a house in Rother Street before finally raising enough money to build a permanent church of their own. Ironically, one of the leading lights was James Cox, junior, son of the James Cox largely responsible for paying for the Payton Street Baptist chapel. Dedicated to St Gregory the Great, the new church was opened out of the town centre on the Warwick Road in 1866. The church and vicarage were designed in the same style by Edward Welby Pugin, the son of the most influential of all nineteenth-century ecclesiastical architects, the tormented genius Augustus Welby Pugin. Unfortunately, although Edward shared some of his father's eccentricities, he did not share many of his architectural talents. St Gregory's is a very tame aisled affair of rusticated stone in a rather mechanical Early English style under a huge pitched roof. The addition of a modern flat-roofed west porch certainly hasn't helped matters.

Public Buildings

After the new town of Stratford was laid out, there were two separate administrations – one for it and one for the old manor. Both were initially dominated by the bishop, but the gradual growth in importance of the Gild of the Holy Cross led to a radical change in local government. Until it was dissolved, the Gild effectively controlled Stratford from its Guildhall, built next to the Gild chapel. The existing building was erected in about 1416–18 and the Gild, and later the Corporation, met in it up until the mid-nineteenth century.

There is some evidence to indicate that this magnificent medieval building extended farther to the north until the Gild chapel was rebuilt at the end of the fifteenth century. On the Church Street façade, the braces in the close-studded timber-framing at the north end are not matched by any at the south end. Inside, the hall itself occupied the rather low ground floor, and there was an over-hall on the jettied floor above, open to the roof and later used by the grammar school.

After the Gild was dissolved the new Corporation took over the ground floor and the reconstituted grammar school appears to have taken over the first floor. Education had been one of the functions carried out by the Church and, in Stratford's case, by the Gild. The original school, built in 1426–7 by the master carpenter John Hessle, was probably the present Pedagogue's House in the school grounds, which are only open to the public by appointment. In the aftermath of the Dissolution many secular schools were founded to fill the educational vacuum,

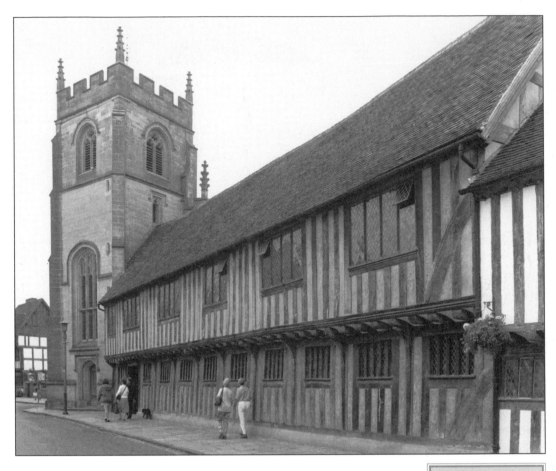

58 The fine Guildhall was built by the powerful Gild of the Holy Cross next to their chapel early in the fifteenth century. It contained two halls, one on each floor, the upper one later becoming part of the grammar school. Its timber-framing was later plastered over and in the mid-nineteenth century it was the fire station, before being restored in the 1890s

which is why there were and are so many King Edward VI and Queen Elizabeth grammar schools. Stratford's King Edward VI's school was simply a reorganization of the older Gild school.

The venerable Guildhall was almost destroyed in the nineteenth century when the ground floor was converted into the town's fire station. By the start of the nineteenth century its framing was covered in plaster and large openings had been pierced in the ground-floor façade to take the horse-drawn fire engines. It was restored to more or less its former state in 1892, the work being paid for by Charles Flower and finished by his younger brother, Edgar. During the work, a long-blocked window was found in the south wall of the lower hall; further restoration in 1949 at first-floor level found another door and

59 Like many similar buildings, Stratford's elegant Palladian-style Town Hall originally had an open ground floor when it was built in 1767, but the arcades were filled in a century later. The building itself was probably designed by Thomas Lightoler and used to be called Shakespeare Hall

window. The discoveries indicate that this building was put up before the adjacent part of the Almshouses. The long, low ground floor with its huge spine beam and large ceiling joists is now the school library. The upper storey, free of any partitions since 1896, is still used for teaching, making it one of the oldest school buildings in the country.

The Town Hall that Garrick helped to finance in the 1760s still stands on the site of the former Bull Ring, despite several alterations and a fire that badly damaged the interior in 1946. It is a rare example in the area of a building made of ashlared stone, that is, stone that is worked to a smooth finish. The stone itself is not a local one, but good-quality Cotswold limestone quarried in the Chipping Campden area. The builder was Robert Newman, although the design is generally considered to be by Timothy Lightoler. It is a good example of the provincial Palladian style, slightly out of date by the time work started in 1767. The principal room, 60 feet by 30 feet, is on the first floor. Originally the ground floor was an open arcade, and it is not too difficult to visualize how it would have looked before the arches were carefully infilled in 1864. At around that time it began to be used for the meetings of the town council and stopped being called by its original name, Shakespeare Hall. Architectural appreciation changes quickly. In 1814 it was described as a 'fine structure of the Tuscan order', but in the early twentieth century, when the picturesque antique was all the rage, as 'undistinguished, not to say wholly unworthy . . . and illustrating the beginning of the least pleasing periods in English architecture.' Now it is once again well respected.

At the opposite end of the High Street from the Town Hall was the original Market Cross. This was virtually derelict by the start of the nineteenth century and a new building was erected in the angle between Henley and Wood streets, looking down the length of Bridge Street. The foundation stone of this new Market House was laid on 19 July 1821, the day of George IV's coronation, and it was quickly finished by William Izod and William Thompson at a cost of just £375. It was a small but rather neat Regency design, with curving flanks perfectly suited to its corner position. Faced with stucco, and topped by a dwarf octagonal clock tower, it originally had an open ground floor, like the Town Hall. This was used for the sale of poultry and dairy produce, while the upstairs space was used for auctions and public events. It was not particularly successful; the ground floor openings were filled in and in 1908 the building was converted into a bank, which it still is.

In the early nineteenth century many towns tried to emulate the fashionable spa towns, such as Bath, Cheltenham and Leamington Spa. A spring at Bishopton, just a mile to the north of Stratford, had been long-held to have medicinal properties, and a small resort opened next to the canal. Officially opened on the future queen's birthday in 1837, it was called the Victoria Spa, one of the very first of many thousands of buildings or monuments literally to be called Victoria. It consisted of a Spa House, bath houses and an hotel, named Green's originally then renamed Queen's. At the time the complex was praised for its 'remarkable degree of taste and liberality' and for the way in which the 'cottage ornée style . . . [was] . . . particularly suited to the character of the scenery around'. Unfortunately, despite

60 The former Market House of 1821 has recently been restored and is now a bank. Small, elegant and stuccoed, it sits happily at the top of Bridge Street and its octagonal cupola-cum-clock tower is a useful landmark. In this case, perhaps, the pretty flower baskets distract from the architecture

61 The story of Stratford's Free Library in Henley Street was an eventful one when it was first planned at the start of this century. The resulting building retains part of a late medieval wing, to the left, with a fine open roof. The rest was virtually rebuilt or newly built

some additions to the hotel soon after it was finished, the spa was not a success. The main buildings still stand, the former hotel being next to a hump-backed canal bridge.

To cater for more common ailments, the new Hospital opened in June 1884, incorporating parts of the dreaded 'Union', the workhouse built in around 1832 to 'serve' the needs of the poor. The Hospital itself is a far friendlier piece of architecture in an attractive neo-vernacular style; the lodge on Arden Street, in a similar vein, was built in 1899.

With the increasing concern for bettering the minds of the population in the nineteenth century, the growth of public libraries became phenomenal and it is difficult now to realize just how rare they once were. The saga of Stratford's Free Library in Henley Street was an eventful one. Andrew Carnegie, a Scot, made a fortune in the USA and spent his old

62 The upstairs of the oldest part of the library is well worth a visit just to see its fine wind-braced roof – but don't disturb the readers!

63 Trinity College, at the end of Church Street, seems to have begun life in the early part of the eighteenth century as a solid Georgian town house. In 1872 the vicar, Dr Collis, converted it into a high-class school for specially selected students. The top storey and pediment were added as part of the rebuilding work. It later became an Army School, and then housed wounded Americans in the First World War

age giving to good causes. Close to his heart was the provision of free libraries, and in 1901 he offered to pay for one to be built in Henley Street on land bought and donated by Archibald Flower. Marie Corelli, as self-appointed guardian of Stratford's architectural heritage, objected to the demolition of the three buildings on the site to make way for the new purpose-built library complex, although it turned out that two of the cottages had been rebuilt in the mid-nineteenth century anyway. Marie stuck to her guns and a compromise solution was found in which the oldest timber-framed portion, possibly of late fifteenth-century date, was restored and the rest virtually rebuilt. The older portion is well worth a visit, especially the upstairs reading room with its fine wind-braced roof.

The quirk of fate that gave Shakespeare to Stratford has resulted in the town having public buildings and monuments specifically dedicated to the man and his work. For nearly two centuries, Americans in particular seem to have been fascinated by both Stratford and Shakespeare, a fascination

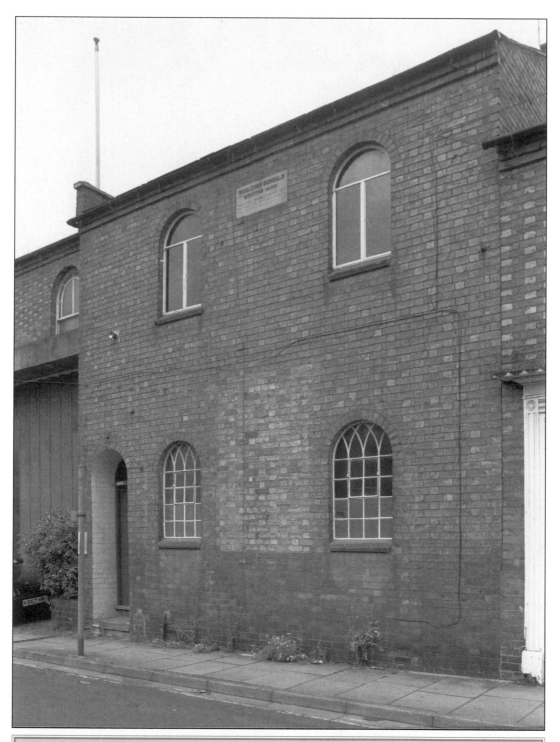

64 The simplicity of the Shakespeare Street Wesleyan Methodist School of 1858 contrasts with the ornate Baptists School in Payton Street built just three years later

65 The new Hospital was opened in June 1884 and built in a rather attractive neo-vernacular style that has now mellowed with age. Behind the new buildings, the site also included much of the once-dreaded Workhouse – usually known as the 'Union' because of the union of parishes that ran it – built about 1832

symbolized by the American Fountain in Rother Square. This was donated to the town by George W. Childs of Philadelphia to celebrate Queen Victoria's Jubilee and was unveiled by no less a person than the famous actor Henry Irving in 1887. The combined clock tower and fountain, with its enthusiastic but totally over-the-top detailing, was designed by Jethro Cossins and looks like the prototype for Walt Disney's fairy castle logo. Its creators obviously struggled to find a suitable watery inscription from the copious works of the 'Swan of Avon', having to make do with 'Honest water which ne'er left man i' the mire' from *Timon of Athens*, not exactly one of Shakespeare's 'greatest hits'.

Across the town, in Bancroft Gardens, is the famous Shakespeare monument designed by Lord Ronald Gower, which was finished in 1888. The bronze Bard looks down from his pedestal at the figures of four of his famous characters – Hamlet,

Prince Hal, Falstaff, and, an odd choice, the evil Lady Macbeth. They represent philosophy, history, comedy and tragedy.

Lord Gower's composition had originally stood next to the first Memorial Theatre. Stratford had no proper theatre until the start of the nineteenth century and that first one proved neither successful nor long-lived. With the increasing interest in all things Shakespearian, it was Charles Flower of the brewery business who promoted the idea of a theatre in the town dedicated to producing Shakespeare's plays. In 1874 a Shakespeare Memorial Association was founded, and in the following year an architectural competition for designs for a new theatre, at a cost of not more than £10,000, was opened. The winning design, out of the twenty-five entries, was by the London partnership of Dodgshun and Unsworth and was built between 1876 and 1879. The main material was brick and the style was a rich, rumbustious neo-Gothic, almost Falstaffian in its opulence and rotundity. Oscar Wilde called it 'a beautiful building, one of the loveliest erected in

67 The playful red-brick Gothic of the Old Bank on Chapel Street is enlivened by terracotta reliefs of scenes from Shakespeare's plays well worth studying. Finished in 1883, it was designed by the Birmingham firm of Harris, Martin & Harris. The panels were by Barfield of Leicester

68 A detail of the terracotta panels of Shakespearian scenes of the Old Bank, designed by Barfield of Leicester

England for many years'. An art gallery and library in the same style were added by Unsworth in 1881.

This rather magnificent pile was not liked by everyone, and Wilde's rival, George Bernard Shaw, is said to have sent a congratulatory telegram when the main auditorium was gutted by fire in March 1926. The old art gallery and library survived, and after many years a fine new theatre, the aptly named Swan, was built within the shell of the old auditorium, opening in 1986. The work has been done with considerable skill and care. From the outside the changes have been minimized, the main problem being the close proximity of the first theatre's much larger successor.

After the 1926 fire an appeal for money for a new theatre was quickly started. Much of the money came from abroad, and from the USA in particular. Again an architectural competition was held, won this time in 1928 by a virtually unknown young woman, 30-year-old Elisabeth Whitworth Scott. Her sole claim to fame was being a cousin of the

69 The intimate Swan Theatre was opened in 1986, a theatre-in-the-round built within the shell of the original Memorial Theatre's auditorium. It recreates in an eminently sensible way the general atmosphere of the Elizabethan venues of Shakespeare's time. The way in which the old has been restored and married to the new is admirable, seen particularly in the former water tower to the left, rebuilt to provide an architectural link between the two buildings

70 The old Memorial Theatre was wonderfully 'over-the-top' in its architecture. There was a definite hint of French château and Rhineland castle. This view is from an early twentieth-century postcard

71 An art gallery and library were added to the original Memorial Theatre in 1881, designed by William Unsworth in the same rich eclectic style. The empty niches and uncarved shields in the façade suggest that the money ran out before it was properly finished, but it is a wonderfully lively piece of work. Happily, it survived the 1926 fire that gutted the main theatre

72 This delightful miniature lodge led to the gardens of the original Memorial Theatre of 1879. It would be rather nice if it could be brought back into use since the present entrance to the new Swan Theatre is rather convoluted

73 The Gothic splendour of the interior of the gallery of the original Memorial Theatre, mercifully spared from the fire that destroyed much of the complex

74 The odd-looking building on the opposite side of Waterside to the main theatre complex must be unique. Built in 1887, it was originally the scene dock, hence the disproportionate height of the central doorway, which allowed the scenery and backdrops to be taken in and out of the building. It later became an electricity sub-station

75 From this angle the
new Memorial Theatre
or Royal Shakespeare
Theatre looks like a
rather ungainly ocean
liner. Whatever its
architectural merits it is
such a well-established
set-piece that it has
become an accepted
national landmark

architect Sir Giles Gilbert Scott; he designed the Anglican
cathedral in Liverpool but, unfortunately, her Royal
Shakespeare Theatre has more in common with another of his
buildings, Battersea Power Station.

The theatre, her only major work, opened in 1932 and was
controversial from the start – a stark, bluff, brick affair that
attracted glowing praise and bitter criticism in roughly equal
measure. A modern design was certainly needed for such an
important building, and it was a worthy attempt. At the time
the architectural critic H.S. Goodhart-Rendel hit the nail right
on the head when he wrote: 'Its style is perhaps a little too
much of the moment to be likely to retain its full relish when
that moment is past'. In retrospect it is let down in many ways
by the ungainly massing of its components and its blandness of
detail. The best view of it, undoubtedly, is from across the
river; and from that angle it does almost look impressive. The
inside is a different story entirely, with form perfectly matched

76 Laurence Williams's Shakespeare Centre, opened in 1964 next to the playwright's birthplace, was a bold, modern design in concrete and glass. Long and low, it acts as a foil to the over-pretty gardens that now occupy what would have been stores and yards connected with John Shakespeare's gloving activities. The recent extensions to the Centre are far less innovative

77 The front of the White Swan on Rother Square owes much to a major remodelling in the 1920s but behind the façade lies an important fifteenth-century building. It originally consisted of a large hall flanked by two cross-wings that slightly project, a plan, because of its shape, known as 'half-H'. When the building was restored, rare wall paintings of Tobit, a character from the Apocrypha, were discovered

to function and excellent facilities for players and playgoers. Although Elisabeth Scott's building is not one of the great masterpieces of twentieth-century English architecture, it has now been in its magnificent riverside setting for nearly seventy years, having been seen by millions and become one of the country's landmarks.

In the Shakespeare Centre, Henley Street, Stratford has a rather unique and fitting public building that is difficult to categorize. Opened in 1964 to celebrate Shakespeare's 400th birthday, it was designed by Laurence Williams for the Birthplace Trust to contain a library, archive, lecture rooms and offices. It was deliberately and uncompromisingly modern, and quite rightly so. The concrete, iron and glass structure may, like the theatre, seem a little dated now, and a little tatty

around the edges, but it was a brave attempt to provide a building worthy of the Trust's academic reputation. It is low enough not to dominate the adjacent Birthplace and its gardens, yet still manages to be a confident and positive piece of architecture. Whether it is likeable or not is a different matter entirely, and possibly an irrelevant one.

The recent extensions to the Centre, opened in 1981, are, it has to be said, far less successful. At the back, facing Guild Street, is a high blank brick wall, while the pseudo-vernacular brick frontage to Henley Street is a disappointing attempt to fit in with the older streetscape. Such a bland and backward-looking style is, in any event, a poor tribute to Shakespeare. He was a great poet, playwright, and, above all, one of the most progressive thinkers of his day, not a quaint bearded character in doublet and hose. If he had been only that, there would have been no need for the Shakespeare Centre at all, and it is very unlikely that Stratford would ever have become the major international tourist destination it now is.

Houses

Considering the terrible fires suffered by Stratford over the years, it is quite surprising just how many medieval houses have survived. None of these appear to date from before the fifteenth century and, oddly, the earliest datable dwellings, the Almshouses in Church Street, are in a terrace. This close-studded timber-framed range, with its jettied upper floor, was built in about 1427 and in the same general style as the slightly earlier Guildhall to the north. Originally, there was a gap between the two, and the present northernmost bay of the Almshouses, although built in the same style as the rest, is clearly slightly later and was added to fill in the gap.

The Almshouses, one of the finest medieval sets in the country, were built by the Gild of the Holy Cross as a Hospice for its retired members and dependents. Twenty-four members in all were housed in small chambers on the two separate floors. By the start of the nineteenth century these twelve men and twelve women were paid 5s a week and had all their clothing free. The timber-framed structure was by this time covered with stucco, and in the process the carved timber shafts that once decorated the main bay posts were cut back. In 1888 three of the Almshouses were restored by Alderman J.J. Nason and the rest were renovated by the start of the 1900s, bringing back to life a part of the magnificent medieval streetscape of Church Street. Between 1981 and 1984 the range was restored again; some of the door-heads are original, but the windows are replacements – and not all in their original places. New, nailed-on, pilaster strips have been attached to the posts – a good idea but they don't look very convincing. The important thing, when all said and done, is that these Almshouses are still being used for the purpose for which they were erected nearly six hundred years ago.

The Almshouses, of course, are not typical of medieval domestic accommodation. Indeed, few of the surviving medieval buildings in the country are. By far the majority of people, particularly in rural areas like Warwickshire, would have been living in quite flimsily constructed buildings that were little more than hovels. The medieval houses that we have been left are mainly those of the relatively prosperous, from yeoman farmer upwards.

By the fifteenth century, most of their houses had three basic elements. The main living room, literally, was the hall, around which a communal life style revolved – eating, talking and, originally, sleeping all took place in it. The late medieval hall was usually open to its great roof and heated by a fire in the central hearth. Smoke from the fire was allowed to find its way, eventually, through a louvre in the top of the roof. Chimneys had been used since Norman times but were slow to

79 Together with the adjacent Guildhall and chapel, the Almshouses in Church Street form one of the most complete early fifteenth-century streetscapes in the country. Unlike its higher-status neighbour, it was originally thatched. Each of the main bay posts originally had attached carved pilasters, but these were cut away when the building was rendered. The timbers were exposed again in 1892

80 Mason's Court in Rother Street is a late medieval 'Wealden' house, probably dating to the late fifteenth century. The recessed portion in the centre was the original hall, open to the roof; to the left the jettied portion was probably the service range, and there was a wider solar range, containing the owner's private rooms, to the right. The building has been extended further to the right and a rear wing added

gain popularity. The entrance to the house was the entrance to the hall, and was usually into a cross-passage across its 'low' end, also known as the screen's passage. Beyond the passage was the service wing, usually built at right angles to the hall and of two storeys, with a chamber on the first floor over store-rooms called the buttery and pantry. The kitchen was usually a completely separate structure close by, because of the ever-present risk of fire. Beyond the 'high' end of the hall, where the owners usually sat, was another two-storey cross-wing, the solar block. This contained the owner's private quarters, usually a parlour on the ground floor and a sleeping chamber on the first.

The overall pattern was often, therefore, a 'half-H' (or 'U') shape, and this can be seen, somewhat fragmentarily, in the White Swan on Rother Square. This was known as the King's House in 1560 and may date back to the mid-fifteenth century. Basically it consisted of a large central hall flanked by two

projecting wings, both of which had jettied first floors. Clearly it has been rebuilt many times, and the former open hall has, like so many, had a first floor inserted into it. When it was last restored, quite radically, in 1927, wall-paintings that depicted scenes from the Apocryphal book of Tobit were discovered. These have been dated to the second half of the sixteenth century, possibly at least a hundred years later than the house itself. In the 1927 restoration, the projecting wings to Rother Square were extended three feet forwards and their timber work is thus completely modern.

In Henley Street, Nos. 41–42 are probably a single late fifteenth-century house with a galleried hall and cross-wing that recent restoration has exposed to view inside, behind an otherwise bland brick façade. This house, the White Swan, and the much-restored Alveston Manor across the river on the Banbury Road, were obviously built for well-to-do people, the first two almost

81 No. 11 Rother Street seems to be another Wealden house, but considerably altered. Notice how the central portion of brickwork has no timbers exposed in it at all, unlike the brickwork on either side. Looking closely, the jettied two-storied service and solar wings can be identified on either side of the original hall. The building is probably of the same general date as Mason's Court nearby – late fifteenth century

certainly for rich merchants. Of particular interest in Stratford is the survival of at least three smaller houses that could be described as being built for the equivalent of the medieval middle class and in a style more usually associated with Kent.

The so-called Wealden house used to be known by architectural historians as the Kentish Yeoman's House because it was of a type built in the hundreds throughout that county. The term Wealden is as equally misleading, for although most of the known examples are in the Weald, there are isolated, but significant, concentrations elsewhere. The most important of these is in Warwickshire, particularly in Coventry, but also in Warwick, Henley-in-Arden and Stratford-upon-Avon. The Wealden is a compact timber-framed structure that has all the main ingredients needed in a late medieval house, but arranged in a very distinctive way. The central open

Above: 83 Nos. 44–45 Wood Street is a fine example of sixteenth-century jettied and close-studded timber-framing, with straight braces introduced into the pattern for added rigidity. The shop fronts blend in well with the building, proving that with a little thought it is still possible to combine good design with commercial necessity

Left: 84 The plain and simple close-studding of No. 2 Sheep Street is typical of the sixteenth century. The way in which the windows lighting the first floor have been raised into miniature dormers is quite clever, adding more light without detracting from the building's character

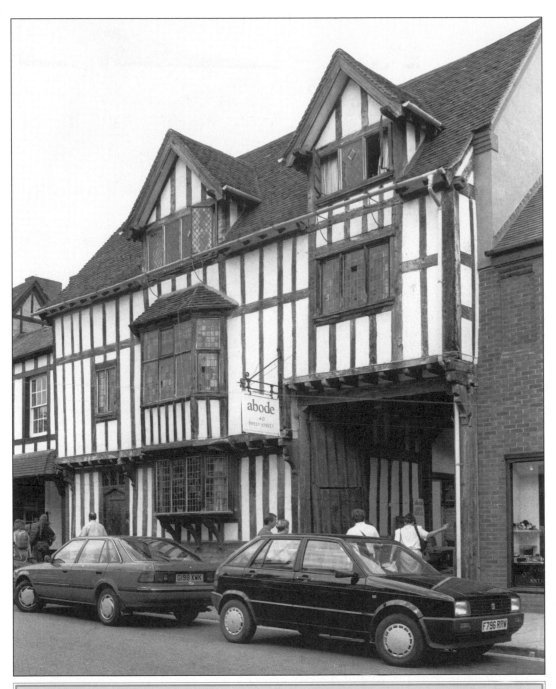

85 The Shrieve's House in Sheep Street is an unusual building. The close-studded ground floor looks reasonably normal sixteenth-century work, but the jettied first floor is astonishingly tall and the style seems later. It has been suggested that the house was rebuilt for William Rogers after the 1595 fire, building on top of the salvaged original ground floor. Rogers was Seargent at the Mace. The house was restored in 1950 and again in 1983

86 Shakespeare's Birthplace is usually dated to the late fifteenth century but this seems too early on stylistic grounds. Recent research has even hinted that the building may date from after Shakespeare's birth, possibly after the fire of 1594. The present appearance owes much to a 1769 engraving, used as a base for the careful restoration of the building between 1857 and 1864

hall is flanked by the solar and service wings in the normal manner. Both wings are jettied at first-floor level, but the hall is not, which means that the upper floors of the wings project farther forward. However, hall and wings are covered by one large single roof. The continuous eaves of the roof run from wing to wing, so that the roof projects farther than the front wall of the hall. The timber carrying the lower slope of the roof at this point is supported by curved braces from the posts of the jettied first floors of the wings, and is sometimes called, rather dramatically, the 'flying bressumer'.

Most of these houses date from the middle of the fifteenth century through to the middle of the sixteenth. Of the three in Stratford, one has been quite confidently dated to the 1480s. This house, Mason's Court on Rother Street, is also the best surviving example in the town. Records suggest that it was built on land owned by the Gild by John Hodgkins within six

87 Anne Hathaway's Cottage, in Shottery, is perhaps the least altered of all the 'Shakespeare' houses, but was never really a cottage. It was a farmstead, parts of which date back to the fifteenth century, though most of the present fabric would have been fairly new when Shakespeare came courting the daughter of the house

88 Hall's Croft, in Old Town, was begun in the early sixteenth century but enlarged a century later by Shakespeare's son-in-law, Dr John Hall. It is another of the Birthplace Trust's properties, and boasts very pleasant gardens

89 Nash's House was the home of Thomas Nash, who married Shakespeare's granddaughter, Elizabeth Hall. In the early nineteenth century it acquired a rather grand neoclassical frontage but this was removed when the timber-framing was radically restored by the Birthplace Trust in about 1912. They had purchased it in 1862, mainly because by that time its garden contained the site of Shakespeare's last home, the long-demolished New Place

90 The Falcon, Chapel Street, is usually dated to around 1500, but the close-studding of its bottom two storeys is almost identical to others nearby rebuilt after the fires of the 1590s. The top storey was probably added in about 1660, when it had become an inn. Later plastered over, and even given stuck-on pilasters, it was restored to its former glory in the 1930s

91 The Tudor House on the corner of Ely Street and Chapel Street is a fine timber-framed pile that once had quite a complex roof structure. It was built at the end of the sixteenth century, replacing one destroyed in the fires, and was altered in the eighteenth century when the roof was heightened

92 In Stratford, Harvard House in High Street is unique. In style it is far more akin to the ornately carved timber-framing of Shropshire or Cheshire. It was built around 1596 for the Rogers family. Katherine Rogers married Robert Harvard of London, and their son, John, emigrated to America, died before he was 30, but left enough money to found Harvard University in 1636. Marie Corelli persuaded Edward Morris of Chicago to pay for it to be restored under her direction in 1907

93 The left-hand building of this pair in Wood Street is a fairly standard timber-framed house of around 1600, with a shallow jetty and close-studding. The one on the right is more unusual – tall, brick, and topped by a shaped Flemish gable. It probably dates to the mid- to late seventeenth century – a time when brick was not quite trusted still; note the skimpy timber-frame in the side wall

94 Clopton House, just
to the north of the town,
was remodelled in the
1660s, when it was
encased in brick. The
pedimented seven-bay
façade fronts a late
sixteenth-century
timber-framed hall

years of 1481. The left-hand cross-wing is still obviously
jettied, but the front of the longer right-hand wing has been
underbuilt with timber-framing, and later extensions have been
added to the rear of the property. No doubt this house, built on
the very edge of the town, was the home of a man more
concerned with the country, possibly a yeoman farmer. Just a
hundred yards or so to the north, and on the same side of the
street, No. 11 Rother Street is also a Wealden house, and of
about the same date, despite its brickwork repairs. In addition,
recent research indicates that No. 13 Henley Street is another,
and there may well be others yet to be rediscovered.

The older medieval domestic arrangements were gradually
altered during the sixteenth century as brick chimneys, wall
fireplaces, and glazed windows became more readily available.
The communal way of domestic life gradually gave way to a
more private one. The insertion of first floors into medieval

open halls was common, and the newer houses were built to a
general layout not too dissimilar to that of the modern house.
The kitchen became part of the main block; the hall gave way
to the parlour or drawing room as the principal 'living' room
and ended up as little more than a lobby; a separate dining
room was provided; and on the upper floors were the
bedchambers and closets. There were, of course, as yet no
bathrooms!

Stratford has many examples of late sixteenth- and early
seventeenth-century houses, though most have been radically
altered over the years as the needs of their occupants changed.
Fortunately, Stratford also has, as a by-product of the
Shakespeare industry, its own 'open-air museum' of buildings
– the far-famed Shakespeare properties. These have all been
restored by the Birthplace Trust as authentically as possible to

96 Mason's Croft on Church Street looks like a fine example of a typical early Georgian brick town house, but actually fronts a largely timber-framed house. In 1901 it was bought and restored by the eccentric novelist Marie Corelli and for a few years was a almost as much a tourist attraction as Shakespeare's Birthplace. It now belongs to the English department of Birmingham University

97 Old Town Place is an early Georgian house with similarities in design to Trinity College just around the corner in Church Street. The window heads and the brick 'aprons' below the lintels are identical and so is the general feel of the building. The door case, although original, is rather unusual and not particularly elegant

98 The pedimented brick façade of No. 1 Old Town dates from about 1760 – and it is not a great surprise to find out that it was added to an earlier timber-framed house

their period appearance and offer a good insight into how such houses looked when the Bard lived.

Mary Arden's House at Wilmcote is a good example of a late medieval house with open hall modernized in the late sixteenth century, but is several miles distant from the town. Anne Hathaway's Cottage at Shottery was also once outside Stratford, but the hamlet, while still retaining much of its independence of character, has been swallowed up by its much larger neighbour. To call the house a cottage is misleading; it is, in fact, a typical yeoman's farmhouse of Shakespeare's period, though parts of it date back to the fifteenth century. Originally called Hewlands, most of the present structure was built in the mid-sixteenth century and later. It was remarkably intact until a fire in 1969 called for quite extensive restoration and repair. On the ground floor is the great parlour (still then called the hall), as well as the

equally spacious kitchen; both have huge fireplaces, typical of the time. The old legend that the young Shakespeare courted Anne by the fire in the hall is irresistible – and, who knows, may even be true. On the upper floors are the bedchambers. The house is probably the least altered of all the properties, partly because the Hathaways continued to live there for many years. The main chimney was rebuilt by John Hathaway in 1697, over a hundred years after William and Anne were married, and much of the furniture on display belonged to the family.

The hallowed Birthplace – always spelt with a capital 'B' – is, from the outside, largely a Victorian recreation, but the interior is much more original. Although it has been dated by some authorities to the late fifteenth century, it seems more likely to be somewhat later. A mid-sixteenth-century

100 Opposite the Guildhall is a splendid example of the refacing of a timber frame. No. 16 Church Street dates to around 1600 and is a typical building of its time and place. The neoclassical Gothick brick front was added for William Hunt in 1768 and remodelled early in the nineteenth century when battlements became popular. The roughcast surprisingly suits it

101 In Guild Street there is a pair of short terraces of the late Georgian period built next to each other. Both were built in 1837 to a basically similar design, but by different builders. Nos. 9–11 Guild Street was built by Joseph Mills and contains three, three-storey houses. Note the use of chequer-patterned brickwork and the neoclassical door surrounds

date seems probable, but recent research has even hinted at the possibility that it was – whisper it softly – built after Shakespeare's birth. It is really two houses, and Shakespeare is believed to have been born in the western one. On its ground floor is the main parlour and the kitchen, both with huge fireplaces, stone-flagged floors, and exposed ceiling beams and joists. The original wooden stairs lead up from the kitchen to the first floor, and to the bedchamber in which the poet was born. All this is laid out with period furniture, though so many tourists and visitors over the centuries have gone away with 'genuine' pieces of Shakespeare's seat, or desk, or bed, that it is difficult to see how any of the original furniture could have survived by the time the Trust took over the building. The other part of the house was used by Shakespeare's father and later became the Swan and Maidenhead. At the rear is a later timber-framed extension.

Hall's Croft is also really two houses, the older part to the

102 Views to the river from the delightful double-decker cast-iron balcony of No. 33 Bridge Street have been ruined by part of a new shopping centre. The mad mix of motifs in the bright white iron work, probably dating from around the 1820s, has a perfect foil in the abundance of colourful flower baskets and troughs. This is the only remnant of Prospect Place

north probably dating to the first half of the sixteenth century. John Hall moved to Stratford in about 1600 and married Shakespeare's daughter, Susanna, in 1607. Possibly after that event, he set about enlarging the house, converting a fairly humble abode into a house fit for the wealthy man that he was. The house was altered several times over the next three hundred years, with bay windows added and older windows enlarged; the timber-framing was covered with render until 1922. Hall's Croft was acquired by the Trust in 1949 and comprehensively restored. It is noted for its walled garden, laid out shortly after the Trust took over but based on Jacobean examples.

The youngest of the Trust's period properties is Nash's House on Chapel Street, once next door to Shakespeare's own long-vanished New Place. Nash married Shakespeare's grand-daughter, Elizabeth Hall, but the house probably dates from just after the 1594 fire. With its three storeys, the upper two jettied, and its more regular appearance both inside and out, it

is very different from the other properties. In fact, the outside appearance dates to about 1912, when a brick front added a century beforehand was taken down. The interior, however, is more or less original. New Place itself was probably the grandest house in Stratford when it was bought by Shakespeare in 1597, but it was largely rebuilt in 1702 and then demolished in 1759.

Changes to the general layout of houses since the seventeenth century have been surprisingly minimal, with the exception of the gradual development of the bathroom, which only became widespread from the early years of the twentieth century. The major changes have really been cosmetic, as architectural fashions here ebbed and flowed. From the later part of the nineteenth century one significant change seen in Stratford, and most other towns, has been the depopulation of the town centres. The middle of towns were overcrowded

105 Many of the timber-framed buildings lining Henley Street were faced in brick in the late eighteenth or early nineteenth century. This row was probably treated in this way in the late eighteenth century, but a glimpse at the side reveals that the range is actually of sixteenth-century date

places well into the nineteenth century, and rich and poor lived cheek-by-jowl. In the late Georgian period there was an attempt to create a better-class area of new brick housing around Payton Street, but it was really in the late nineteenth and early twentieth centuries that more and more of those that could afford it left for the leafy new suburbs. A traditional way of life going back centuries slowly petered out. Architecturally, it meant that the grander houses in the centre became run down and subdivided, and later, the upper floors of houses in which tradesmen had lived 'over the shop' were converted to offices or storerooms, or simply left empty.

Writing at the start of this century, A.G. Bradley noted that Stratford was

skirted by quite a thick margin of roads and avenues of red

106 Newlands Almshouses on Guild Street were founded by Mary Newland, for women. The present neo-Tudor buildings were finished in 1857, and despite appearances to the contrary, there are actually four separate houses in the short terrace

107 Wonderfully bold and brash, these houses on Arden Street have a name as daft as their architecture – Glencoe Terrace. The row was designed by Carey & Findon and finished in 1869 in High Victorian 'Domestic Gothic'. No doubt very serious at the time, it now looks very silly, but great fun!

brick villas, not aesthetically offensive, but just the ordinary residential quarter that springs up around county towns now that tradesmen no longer live over their shops, but, like the professional and wholesale trading element, grow roses or play tennis upon their own half acre in the suburbs.

In Stratford, it was not just the traders that went to live in the suburbs; commuters to Birmingham and Coventry came to live in the town and used the railway, and others retired to it. Few did so in a grander way than Mark Philips, who belonged to one of the Manchester cotton dynasties. He commissioned Henry Clutton, better known for his Roman Catholic churches, to design a new house just outside the town and not far from Clopton House. The result, Welcombe House, is a huge exercise in the 'neo-Jacobethan', bristling with shaped gables, batteries of chimney stacks and massive bay windows. The

108 Concern grew in the nineteenth century about the condition of working-class housing in towns throughout England. Local companies or trusts were formed to help matters. The Stratford-upon-Avon Labourers Dwellings Co. Ltd built two nearly identical terraces – one in Mansell Street in 1876 and, in the following year, this terrace around the corner in Arden Street

109 The Welcombe House Hotel began life as the home of Mark Philips, a Manchester cotton magnate. The neo-Jacobethan pile was designed by Henry Clutton and the first part completed in 1867. It has been a hotel for many years, and it is nice to see that the gardens have been restored

110 At first glance this brick terrace, Nos. 60–72 Birmingham Road, with its overhanging monopitched roof and simple lines, could easily be mistaken for a typical 1960s' development. The seven dwellings were actually designed as early as 1938 by F.R.S. Yorke, who was also responsible for the early Gatwick Airport buildings

first part was finished in 1867, and more was added in the early 1900s.

Throughout this century these trends have continued as the town's deserved popularity has grown, and the recent opening of the M40 motorway has made commuting from Stratford that much more convenient. From the late 1980s onwards the huge demand for accommodation in the town has been met not only by new houses, but also by that decidedly un-English form of housing, the apartment block.

Industrial Buildings and Bridges

Stratford has mainly been a trading rather than a manufacturing town. Those industries that it did have were all connected with the local agricultural produce. Nothing obvious survives of the weaving and thread-making industry that thrived until the end of the sixteenth century, apart from the legacy of the houses of the merchants that profited by it. Now very little survives of the brewing industry that was established in the town for centuries.

The first bridge over the Avon at Stratford was probably built upstream from the original ford at about the same time as the new borough was being laid out. In 1235 there is a mention of Richard the Bridgekeeper, and in 1269 the first reference to the 'Great Bridge' itself. This would have been a timber bridge, subject to constant repair and rebuilding. At one end there was a chapel dedicated to St Mary Magdalene and endowed with land to provide the money to keep the bridge in good order. The chapel was looked after by a hermit; in the time of Henry VI this obviously quite important post was held by one Henry Rawlins, a member of the Gild of the Holy Cross. By the end of the fifteenth century the bridge was 'very smaulle and ille . . . a poore bridge of tymber, and no causey to come to it'. Some people even refused to use it, fearing for their safety.

Sir Hugh Clopton then paid for 'the great and sumptuose

bridge' with its '14 great archis of stone, and a longe causey made of stone and now waullyed on eche syde', finished in about 1490 and so admired by Leland fifty years later. Altogether there were nineteen arches originally, five smaller ones being under the causeway, and the total length of the structure was 376 yards. It is a credit to the master mason involved that it is still a vital transport link over 500 years later and puts up with the thousands of motor vehicles that use it every day.

The bridge was badly damaged by flooding in 1588, when an arch at either end was washed away. In the Civil War it was the only reason why either side took any notice of Stratford, and the Parliament ordered the destruction of one of the main arches. The bridge was originally only 16 feet wide. In the

112 Five hundred years after it was built Hugh Clopton's Great Bridge still carries all the traffic heading into Stratford from the south. It was widened on the upstream side in 1814, and the cast-iron cantilevered footpath was added in 1827. The downstream side looks more or less the same as it did when it was built

brief heyday of the stage coach Stratford was an important route centre but the width of the bridge was, not surprisingly, considered to be a hindrance to traffic. In 1812 an Act of Parliament allowed the Corporation to charge tolls to pay for the upkeep of the bridge, and for its widening. The road width was increased by adding narrow arches to the masonry on the upstream side, the work being directed by an engineer called Mr Mackintosh. The cast-iron cantilevered footpath, also on the upstream side, was installed in 1827 for the convenience of pedestrians. It was cast at the Eagle Foundry of Smith & Hawkes in Birmingham.

Running parallel to the Clopton Bridge, and just downstream from it, is the nine-arched brick pedestrian bridge that most visitors to Stratford will probably use sooner or later. Free from traffic, it provides a safe and convenient link from the Bancroft Gardens to the playing fields and attractions on the other bank, as well as offering splendid views of the town, the busy riverscape, and the Memorial

114 A gentle stroll alongside the Stratford Canal is well worth the effort. The canal opened in 1816 but by the 1930s was derelict. Plans to close it were halted by local pressure and it was eventually reopened in 1961. It is now leased by the National Trust

Theatre. Few people will realize at first that this is actually a railway bridge, or, more correctly, a tramway bridge. The Stratford & Moreton Tramway was first mooted soon after the canal was completed, and was authorized in 1821. It was promoted, surveyed and mainly financed by William James, who had finished the canal, with help from a Mr Kershaw of Lapworth.

The bridge was ready by 1823 and the horse-drawn line was finished three years later, ending in a series of sidings on the canalside wharves nearby. Thus three modes of transport – river, canal and tramway – were all interconnected in an eminently sensible way that seems beyond today's traffic planners. The tramway had fallen out of use by the end of the century and the rails were lifted in 1918 to help the war effort. The bridge was then converted to the invaluable pedestrian crossing it now is, and a restored wagon at the town end is a reminder of the past. It is a rather pleasant structure, of honest proportions, and few people today would agree with an

115 The Stratford &
Moreton Tramway was
opened in 1826 but the
brick tramway bridge
across the Avon was
completed some time
beforehand. The horse-
drawn tramway closed
towards the end of the
nineteenth century and
the tracks were lifted in
the First World War. The
bridge is now a vital
pedestrian link

assessment made of it shortly after it was opened. It was then described as 'a brick bridge, claiming no pretensions to architecture, and sadly detracting from the beauty of the expanding river'.

Although the Avon had probably been navigable at certain water levels for centuries, it was not a reliable transport artery until the seventeenth century. Tradition has it that the Earl of Warwick in Henry VI's time first put forward a plan to improve the river all the way from Coventry downstream to its confluence with the Severn at Tewkesbury. William Sandys obtained his Act of Parliament to make the Avon navigable to the town in 1636. It is possible that barges of up to 30 tons were able to reach the town by 1639, but the engineering works were not quite complete at the outbreak of the Civil War. The navigation was abandoned and presumably became derelict, for in 1667 Andrew Yarranton is known to have

116 At the town end of the Tramway Bridge is Tramway House, probably built at the same time as the bridge to house an official of the line

117 One of the wagons
that used the tramway
has been restored and
now stands on its
original 'fiah-bellied'
cast-iron rails near the
bridge. The rails were
fixed to stone blocks.
Note the rather primitive
braking system

repaired the work and completed the waterway, and was thinking about his grand new towns. Barges carrying up to 40 tons could now reach Stratford, improving the town's status as a trading and market centre. Bancroft and Swan's Nest wharves, on opposite sides of the river, thrived. The river continued to be quite busy throughout the eighteenth century, even though later on it was described as being 'Subject to Floods & Drought which makes the Passage difficult and tedious'. Traffic declined rapidly in the early years of the nineteenth century, a situation explained by a writer in 1829: 'at present, however, in consequence of the numerous canals, and the unparalleled improvements of the turnpike roads, the trade by water is considerable diminished'.

Stratford's own canal took a long time to build, and has had an eventful life, but few canals in Britain can have such an attractive terminus, meeting the Avon at the basin in Bancroft

118 A late seventeenth-century dovecote stands as the sole survivor of a farmstead that once stood on Rother Street, but it does show just how important rural life was to the town even at that date, and how agriculture was an integral part of its economy

119 Cox's timber yard has been by the canal basin for many years and the drying sheds where timber matured probably date from the mid-nineteenth century. It is really pleasing to see this type of activity still being carried on right in the middle of a tourist town

Gardens. It was certainly not always like this, for all this area was once taken up with canalside warehouses and industry. There was another large basin closer to the site of the Memorial Theatre as well, and the whole area would have been full of bustle and noise after the canal opened, officially, on 24 June 1816. The tramway at first complemented the canal, and there were high hopes that Stratford was 'likely to become a busy and thriving little port'.

The arrival of steam railways later on brought about the demise of both canal and tramway. By 1930 the canal was derelict and in 1958 plans were drawn up to abandon it officially and fill it in. Local pressure eventually led to the National Trust leasing it in 1961 and three years of hard work resulted in its restoration. A walk along the canal towpath from Bancroft to Bishopton gives a very different view of the town, well away from the tourist bustle.

Further Reading

Local Books

Bearman, R., *Stratford-upon-Avon as it Was* (1984)

Fogg, N., *Stratford-upon-Avon: Portrait of a Town* (1986)

Fox, L., *In Honour of Shakespeare* (1972)

Hadfield, C. and Norris, J., *Waterways to Stratford* (1968)

General Books

Brunskill, R.W., *Timber Building in Britain* (1985)

Brunskill, R.W., *Brick Building in Britain* (1990)

Clifton-Taylor, A., *A Pattern of English Building* (4th ed. 1987)

Cruickshank, D., *A Guide to the Georgian Buildings of Britain and Ireland* (1985)

Harris, R., *Discovering Timber-framed Buildings* (1978)

Pevsner, N., *The Buildings of England* series, in county volumes

Platt, C., *The English Medieval Town* (1976)

Index